Morning
Mindset

GRIT JOURNALS

ISBN-10: 1982062614
ISBN-13: 978-1982062613

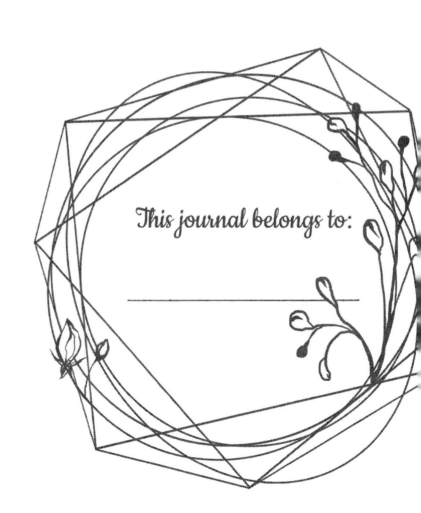

This journal belongs to:

_____

What you do first thing in the morning affects your whole day.
What you do every day affects your whole life.

Morning Mindset is a daily journal designed to help you create a life you're proud of.

This journal includes 13 weeks of morning pages that you can fill out after you wake up, and weekly check-in forms to help you reflect and plan.

With regular use of this journal, soon you'll feel more grateful, purposeful and satisfied with your life.

How To Use This Journal?

Today's word – Pick a word or phrase that will define your day.

How am I feeling right now? – Are you feeling motivated, happy, in love, frustrated, or don't even want to leave your bed? Track your mood every morning before you do anything else, and see how your actions during the day affect it.

Gratitude – Learn to appreciate life! Every morning, think of at least 3 things you're grateful for. Soon you'll realize that even on your worst days, there's something to appreciate.

Join our Facebook Daily Gratitude Group at
gritjournals.com/grateful

Why is it worth waking up today? – Every day is a new opportunity for something amazing. You will never get this day back, so better make it count.

What did I do for my growth yesterday? – Personal growth doesn't happen overnight; you need to work on it every single day. Having to write down what you did for your growth the day before helps keep you accountable and it's a great reminder that you should be making active effort every day on your personal development.

My goals for today – Be more purposeful by planning your day ahead. Use it as a checklist during your day. There's nothing like celebrating a task done by being able to physically check it off.

Weekly check-in – Track your progress and how you feel about the past week. Look through your previous responses to understand why you feel that way.

What did I learn from this week? – We learn something new every single day. Being aware of the lessons we learn and writing them down helps us grow.

My Values

....

....

....

....

....

....

....

....

....

....

....

....

"Do One Thing Every Day That Scares You."

— Eleanor Roosevelt

Date: .... *Today's word:* ....

How am I feeling right now?

....

I'm grateful for...

....

....

....

Why is it worth waking up today?

....

What did I do for my growth yesterday?

....

What didn't work yesterday?

....

My goals for today:

☐ .... ☐ ....

☐ .... ☐ ....

"If the only prayer you ever say in your entire life is thank you, it will be enough."

– Meister Eckhart

Date: .... | *Today's word:* ....

How am I feeling right now?

....

I'm grateful for...

....

....

....

Why is it worth waking up today?

....

What did I do for my growth yesterday?

....

What didn't work yesterday?

....

My goals for today:

☐ ....   ☐ ....

☐ ....   ☐ ....

"Gratitude is not only the greatest of virtues, but the parent of all other."

– Marcus Tullius Cicero

Date: .... *Today's word:* ....

How am I feeling right now?

....

I'm grateful for...

....

....

....

Why is it worth waking up today?

....

What did I do for my growth yesterday?

....

What didn't work yesterday?

....

My goals for today:

☐ .... ☐ ....

☐ .... ☐ ....

"Happiness is a habit—cultivate it."

– Albert Hubbard

Date: .... *Today's word:*........................

How am I feeling right now?

....

I'm grateful for…

....

....

....

Why is it worth waking up today?

....

What did I do for my growth yesterday?

....

What didn't work yesterday?

....

My goals for today:

☐ .... ☐ ....

☐ .... ☐ ....

"For every minute you are angry you lose sixty seconds of happiness."

– Ralph Waldo Emerson

Date: .... | *Today's word:* ....

How am I feeling right now?

....

I'm grateful for…

....

....

....

Why is it worth waking up today?

....

What did I do for my growth yesterday?

....

What didn't work yesterday?

....

My goals for today:

☐ .... ☐ ....

☐ .... ☐ ....

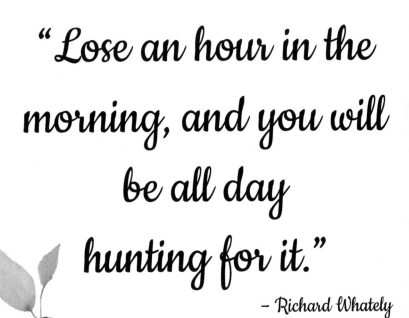

"Lose an hour in the morning, and you will be all day hunting for it."

– Richard Whately

Date: .... *Today's word:* ....

How am I feeling right now?

....

I'm grateful for…

....

....

....

Why is it worth waking up today?

....

What did I do for my growth yesterday?

....

What didn't work yesterday?

....

My goals for today:

☐ .... ☐ ....

☐ .... ☐ ....

"Be the type of person you want to meet."

– Unknown

Date: .... | *Today's word:* ....

How am I feeling right now?

....

I'm grateful for…

....

....

....

Why is it worth waking up today?

....

What did I do for my growth yesterday?

....

What didn't work yesterday?

....

My goals for today:

☐ .... ☐ ....

☐ .... ☐ ....

Weekly Check-in

How satisfied am I with my previous week?

0   1   2   3   4   5   6   7   8   9   10

What did I learn from this week?

....

....

....

....

What do I want to achieve next week?

....

....

....

....

Loving Morning Mindset?

Please support us by leaving a review on Amazon

Use the hashtag **#gritjournals** when you post on Instagram!

"Happiness is when what you think, what you say, and what you do are in harmony."

– Mahatma Gandhi

Date: .... | *Today's word:* ....

How am I feeling right now?

....

I'm grateful for...

....

....

....

Why is it worth waking up today?

....

What did I do for my growth yesterday?

....

What didn't work yesterday?

....

My goals for today:

☐ .... ☐ ....

☐ .... ☐ ....

"There is nothing either good or bad, but thinking makes it so."

– William Shakespeare

Date: .... | *Today's word:* ....

How am I feeling right now?

....

I'm grateful for…

....

....

....

Why is it worth waking up today?

....

What did I do for my growth yesterday?

....

What didn't work yesterday?

....

My goals for today:

☐ .... ☐ ....

☐ .... ☐ ....

"*Love, the poet said,*
is woman's whole
existence."

– Virginia Woolf

Date: .... *Today's word:* ....

How am I feeling right now?

....

I'm grateful for…

....

....

....

Why is it worth waking up today?

....

What did I do for my growth yesterday?

....

What didn't work yesterday?

....

My goals for today:

☐ .... ☐ ....

☐ .... ☐ ....

"We must have perseverance and above all confidence in ourselves."

– Marie Curie

Date: .... | *Today's word:* ....

How am I feeling right now?

....

I'm grateful for...

....

....

....

Why is it worth waking up today?

....

What did I do for my growth yesterday?

....

What didn't work yesterday?

....

My goals for today:

☐ .... ☐ ....

☐ .... ☐ ....

"The mystery of human existence lies not in just staying alive, but in finding something to live for."

– Fyodor Dostoyevsky

Date: .... | *Today's word:* ....

How am I feeling right now?

....

I'm grateful for…

....

....

....

Why is it worth waking up today?

....

What did I do for my growth yesterday?

....

What didn't work yesterday?

....

My goals for today:

☐ .... ☐ ....

☐ .... ☐ ....

"No one can make
you feel inferior
without your consent."

– Eleanor Roosevelt

Date: ....   *Today's word:* ....

How am I feeling right now?

....

I'm grateful for…

....

....

....

Why is it worth waking up today?

....

What did I do for my growth yesterday?

....

What didn't work yesterday?

....

My goals for today:

☐ ....   ☐ ....

☐ ....   ☐ ....

"Success is the sum of small efforts – repeated day in and day out."

– Robert Collier

Date: .... | *Today's word:* ....

How am I feeling right now?

....

I'm grateful for…

....

....

....

Why is it worth waking up today?

....

What did I do for my growth yesterday?

....

What didn't work yesterday?

....

My goals for today:

☐ .... ☐ ....

☐ .... ☐ ....

Weekly Check-in

How satisfied am I with my previous week?

0   1   2   3   4   5   6   7   8   9   10

What did I learn from this week?

....

....

....

....

What do I want to achieve next week?

....

....

....

....

"Look deep into nature,
and then you will
understand everything
better."

– Albert Einstein

Date: .... | *Today's word:* ....

How am I feeling right now?

....

I'm grateful for…

....

....

....

Why is it worth waking up today?

....

What did I do for my growth yesterday?

....

What didn't work yesterday?

....

My goals for today:

☐ .... ☐ ....

☐ .... ☐ ....

"If everyone is thinking alike, then no one is thinking."

– Benjamin Franklin

Date: .... | *Today's word:* ....

How am I feeling right now?

....

I'm grateful for...

....

....

....

Why is it worth waking up today?

....

What did I do for my growth yesterday?

....

What didn't work yesterday?

....

My goals for today:

☐ .... ☐ ....

☐ .... ☐ ....

"As is a tale, so is life: not how long it is, but how good it is, is what matters."

– Seneca

Date: .... *Today's word:* ....

How am I feeling right now?

....

I'm grateful for...

....

....

....

Why is it worth waking up today?

....

What did I do for my growth yesterday?

....

What didn't work yesterday?

....

My goals for today:

☐ ....   ☐ ....

☐ ....   ☐ ....

"The best way to cheer yourself is to try to cheer someone else up."

– Mark Twain

Date: .... | *Today's word:*.......................

How am I feeling right now?

....

I'm grateful for…

....

....

....

Why is it worth waking up today?

....

What did I do for my growth yesterday?

....

What didn't work yesterday?

....

My goals for today:

☐ .... ☐ ....

☐ .... ☐ ....

"Tomorrow is always fresh, with no mistakes in it."

– Lucy Maud Montgomery

Date: ....   *Today's word:* ....

How am I feeling right now?

....

I'm grateful for...

....

....

....

Why is it worth waking up today?

....

What did I do for my growth yesterday?

....

What didn't work yesterday?

....

My goals for today:

☐ ....   ☐ ....

☐ ....   ☐ ....

"Use the occasion, for it passes swiftly."

– Ovid

Date: .... | *Today's word:* ....

How am I feeling right now?

....

I'm grateful for...

....

....

....

Why is it worth waking up today?

....

What did I do for my growth yesterday?

....

What didn't work yesterday?

....

My goals for today:

☐ .... ☐ ....

☐ .... ☐ ....

"Forever – is
composed of Nows."

– Emily Dickinson

Date: .... | *Today's word:* ....

How am I feeling right now?

....

I'm grateful for…

....

....

....

Why is it worth waking up today?

....

What did I do for my growth yesterday?

....

What didn't work yesterday?

....

My goals for today:

☐ .... ☐ ....

☐ .... ☐ ....

Weekly Check-in

How satisfied am I with my previous week?

0   1   2   3   4   5   6   7   8   9   10

What did I learn from this week?

....

....

....

....

What do I want to achieve next week?

....

....

....

....

"Well done is better than well said."

– Benjamin Franklin

Date: .... | *Today's word:* ....

How am I feeling right now?

....

I'm grateful for…

....

....

....

Why is it worth waking up today?

....

What did I do for my growth yesterday?

....

What didn't work yesterday?

....

My goals for today:

☐ .... ☐ ....

☐ .... ☐ ....

"Be yourself; everyone else is already taken."

– Oscar Wilde

Date:........................ | *Today's word:*........................

How am I feeling right now?

....

I'm grateful for…

....

....

....

Why is it worth waking up today?

....

What did I do for my growth yesterday?

....

What didn't work yesterday?

....

My goals for today:

☐ .... ☐ ....

☐ .... ☐ ....

"A person who never made a mistake never tried anything new."

– Albert Einstein

Date:........................ | *Today's word:*.......................

How am I feeling right now?

....

I'm grateful for…

....

....

....

Why is it worth waking up today?

....

What did I do for my growth yesterday?

....

What didn't work yesterday?

....

My goals for today:

☐ .... ☐ ....

☐ .... ☐ ....

"Think of all the beauty still left around you and be happy."

– Anne Frank

Date: .... | *Today's word:* ....

How am I feeling right now?

....

I'm grateful for…

....

....

....

Why is it worth waking up today?

....

What did I do for my growth yesterday?

....

What didn't work yesterday?

....

My goals for today:

☐ .... ☐ ....

☐ .... ☐ ....

"Time wasted is existence; used is life."

– Edward Young

Date: .... *Today's word:* ....

How am I feeling right now?

....

I'm grateful for…

....

....

....

Why is it worth waking up today?

....

What did I do for my growth yesterday?

....

What didn't work yesterday?

....

My goals for today:

☐ .... ☐ ....

☐ .... ☐ ....

"Lost time can never be found again."

– Benjamin Franklin

Date: .... *Today's word:* ....

How am I feeling right now?

....

I'm grateful for…

....

....

....

Why is it worth waking up today?

....

What did I do for my growth yesterday?

....

What didn't work yesterday?

....

My goals for today:

☐ ....   ☐ ....

☐ ....   ☐ ....

"Begin while others are procrastinating. Work while others are wishing."

– William Arthur Ward

Date: .... *Today's word:* ....

How am I feeling right now?

....

I'm grateful for...

....

....

....

Why is it worth waking up today?

....

What did I do for my growth yesterday?

....

What didn't work yesterday?

....

My goals for today:

☐ .... ☐ ....

☐ .... ☐ ....

Weekly Check-in

How satisfied am I with my previous week?

0   1   2   3   4   5   6   7   8   9   10

What did I learn from this week?

....

....

....

....

What do I want to achieve next week?

....

....

....

....

"Books are the mirrors of the soul."

– Virginia Woolf

Date: .... | *Today's word:* ....

How am I feeling right now?

....

I'm grateful for…

....

....

....

Why is it worth waking up today?

....

What did I do for my growth yesterday?

....

What didn't work yesterday?

....

My goals for today:

☐ .... ☐ ....

☐ .... ☐ ....

"The only difference between success and failure is the ability to take action."

– Alexandre Graham Bell

Date: .... *Today's word:* ....

How am I feeling right now?

....

I'm grateful for...

....

....

....

Why is it worth waking up today?

....

What did I do for my growth yesterday?

....

What didn't work yesterday?

....

My goals for today:

☐ .... ☐ ....

☐ .... ☐ ....

"Quality is not an act, it is a habit."

– Aristotle

Date: .... *Today's word:*........................

How am I feeling right now?

....

I'm grateful for…

....

....

....

Why is it worth waking up today?

....

What did I do for my growth yesterday?

....

What didn't work yesterday?

....

My goals for today:

☐ .... ☐ ....

☐ .... ☐ ....

"Be as you wish

to seem."

– Socrates

Date: .... *Today's word:* ....

How am I feeling right now?

....

I'm grateful for…

....

....

....

Why is it worth waking up today?

....

What did I do for my growth yesterday?

....

What didn't work yesterday?

....

My goals for today:

☐ .... ☐ ....

☐ .... ☐ ....

"The future is purchased by the present."

– Samuel Johnson

Date: .... | *Today's word:* ....

How am I feeling right now?

....

I'm grateful for...

....

....

....

Why is it worth waking up today?

....

What did I do for my growth yesterday?

....

What didn't work yesterday?

....

My goals for today:

☐ .... ☐ ....

☐ .... ☐ ....

"Faith in oneself is the best and safest course."

– Michelangelo

Date: ....   *Today's word:* ....

How am I feeling right now?

....

I'm grateful for…

....

....

....

Why is it worth waking up today?

....

What did I do for my growth yesterday?

....

What didn't work yesterday?

....

My goals for today:

☐ ....   ☐ ....

☐ ....   ☐ ....

"Believe you can
and you're halfway
there."

– Theodore Roosevelt

Date: ....   *Today's word:* ....

How am I feeling right now?

....

I'm grateful for...

....

....

....

Why is it worth waking up today?

....

What did I do for my growth yesterday?

....

What didn't work yesterday?

....

My goals for today:

☐ ....   ☐ ....

☐ ....   ☐ ....

Weekly Check-in

How satisfied am I with my previous week?

0   1   2   3   4   5   6   7   8   9   10

What did I learn from this week?

....

....

....

....

What do I want to achieve next week?

....

....

....

....

"The only true wisdom
is in knowing you
know nothing."

– Socrates

Date: .... | *Today's word:* ....

How am I feeling right now?

....

I'm grateful for…

....

....

....

Why is it worth waking up today?

....

What did I do for my growth yesterday?

....

What didn't work yesterday?

....

My goals for today:

☐ .... ☐ ....

☐ .... ☐ ....

"*Life is ours to be spent, not to be saved.*"

– D. H. Lawrence

Date: ....   *Today's word:*.....................

How am I feeling right now?

....

I'm grateful for…

....

....

....

Why is it worth waking up today?

....

What did I do for my growth yesterday?

....

What didn't work yesterday?

....

My goals for today:

☐ .... ☐ ....

☐ .... ☐ ....

"Everything flows, and
nothing abides,
everything gives way,
and nothing stays fixed."

– Heraclitus

Date: .... | *Today's word:* ....

How am I feeling right now?

....

I'm grateful for…

....

....

....

Why is it worth waking up today?

....

What did I do for my growth yesterday?

....

What didn't work yesterday?

....

My goals for today:

☐ .... ☐ ....

☐ .... ☐ ....

"I would rather die of passion than of boredom."

— Vincent van Gogh

Date: .... | *Today's word:* ....

How am I feeling right now?

....

I'm grateful for…

....

....

....

Why is it worth waking up today?

....

What did I do for my growth yesterday?

....

What didn't work yesterday?

....

My goals for today:

☐ .... ☐ ....

☐ .... ☐ ....

"You must do the things you think you cannot do."

– Eleanor Roosevelt

Date: .... *Today's word:* ....

How am I feeling right now?

....

I'm grateful for…

....

....

....

Why is it worth waking up today?

....

What did I do for my growth yesterday?

....

What didn't work yesterday?

....

My goals for today:

☐ ....   ☐ ....

☐ ....   ☐ ....

"Learning is not attained by chance, it must be sought for with ardor and diligence."

– Abigail Adams

Date: .... *Today's word:* ....

How am I feeling right now?

....

I'm grateful for…

....

....

....

Why is it worth waking up today?

....

What did I do for my growth yesterday?

....

What didn't work yesterday?

....

My goals for today:

☐ .... ☐ ....

☐ .... ☐ ....

"Self-education is, I firmly believe, the only kind of education there is."

– Isaac Asimov

Date: ....   *Today's word:* ....

How am I feeling right now?

....

I'm grateful for…

....

....

....

Why is it worth waking up today?

....

What did I do for my growth yesterday?

....

What didn't work yesterday?

....

My goals for today:

☐ ....   ☐ ....

☐ ....   ☐ ....

Weekly Check-in

· ·

How satisfied am I with my previous week?

0   1   2   3   4   5   6   7   8   9   10

What did I learn from this week?

....

....

....

....

What do I want to achieve next week?

....

....

....

....

"Giving is living.
If you stop wanting to give, there's nothing more to live for."

– Audrey Hepburn

Date: .... *Today's word:* ....

How am I feeling right now?

....

I'm grateful for...

....

....

....

Why is it worth waking up today?

....

What did I do for my growth yesterday?

....

What didn't work yesterday?

....

My goals for today:

☐ .... ☐ ....

☐ .... ☐ ....

"Great minds discuss ideas; average minds discuss events; small minds discuss people."

– Eleanor Roosevelt

Date: ....   *Today's word:* ....

How am I feeling right now?

....

I'm grateful for…

....

....

....

Why is it worth waking up today?

....

What did I do for my growth yesterday?

....

What didn't work yesterday?

....

My goals for today:

☐ ....   ☐ ....

☐ ....   ☐ ....

"Anyone who stops learning is old, whether at twenty or eighty."

– Henry Ford

Date: ....   *Today's word:* ....

How am I feeling right now?

....

I'm grateful for…

....

....

....

Why is it worth waking up today?

....

What did I do for my growth yesterday?

....

What didn't work yesterday?

....

My goals for today:

☐ ....   ☐ ....

☐ ....   ☐ ....

"The happiness of your life depends upon the quality of your thoughts."

– Marcus Aurelius

Date: .... *Today's word:* ....

How am I feeling right now?

....

I'm grateful for…

....

....

....

Why is it worth waking up today?

....

What did I do for my growth yesterday?

....

What didn't work yesterday?

....

My goals for today:

☐ ....   ☐ ....

☐ ....   ☐ ....

"What we think,
we become."

– The Buddha

Date:........................ *Today's word:*........................

How am I feeling right now?

....

I'm grateful for…

....

....

....

Why is it worth waking up today?

....

What did I do for my growth yesterday?

....

What didn't work yesterday?

....

My goals for today:

☐ .... ☐ ....

☐ .... ☐ ....

"We must believe that we are gifted for something, and that this thing, at whatever cost, must be attained."

– Marie Curie

Date: .... | *Today's word:*........................

How am I feeling right now?

....

I'm grateful for…

....

....

....

Why is it worth waking up today?

....

What did I do for my growth yesterday?

....

What didn't work yesterday?

....

My goals for today:

☐ .... ☐ ....

☐ .... ☐ ....

"Everyone needs to be valued. Everyone has the potential to give something back."

– Princess Diana

Date: .... | *Today's word:* ....

How am I feeling right now?

....

I'm grateful for...

....

....

....

Why is it worth waking up today?

....

What did I do for my growth yesterday?

....

What didn't work yesterday?

....

My goals for today:

☐ ....   ☐ ....

☐ ....   ☐ ....

Weekly Check-in

How satisfied am I with my previous week?

0   1   2   3   4   5   6   7   8   9   10

What did I learn from this week?

....

....

....

....

What do I want to achieve next week?

....

....

....

....

"We are what we repeatedly do. Excellence, then, is not an act, but a habit."

– Will Durant

Date: .... *Today's word:* ....

How am I feeling right now?

....

I'm grateful for...

....

....

....

Why is it worth waking up today?

....

What did I do for my growth yesterday?

....

What didn't work yesterday?

....

My goals for today:

☐ .... ☐ ....

☐ .... ☐ ....

"Whether you think you can or you think you can't, you're right."

– Henry Ford

Date: .... | *Today's word:*........................

How am I feeling right now?

....

I'm grateful for…

....

....

....

Why is it worth waking up today?

....

What did I do for my growth yesterday?

....

What didn't work yesterday?

....

My goals for today:

☐ .... ☐ ....

☐ .... ☐ ....

"If you try to cure evil with evil you will add more pain to your fate."

– Sophocles

Date: .... | *Today's word:* ....

How am I feeling right now?

....

I'm grateful for...

....

....

....

Why is it worth waking up today?

....

What did I do for my growth yesterday?

....

What didn't work yesterday?

....

My goals for today:

☐ .... ☐ ....

☐ .... ☐ ....

"Never give up on a dream just because of the time it will take to accomplish it. The time will pass anyway."

— Earl Nightingale

Date: .... Today's word: ....

How am I feeling right now?

....

I'm grateful for…

....

....

....

Why is it worth waking up today?

....

What did I do for my growth yesterday?

....

What didn't work yesterday?

....

My goals for today:

☐ .... ☐ ....

☐ .... ☐ ....

"Genius is one percent inspiration and ninety-nine percent perspiration."

– Thomas Edison

Date: .... *Today's word:* ....

How am I feeling right now?

....

I'm grateful for…

....

....

....

Why is it worth waking up today?

....

What did I do for my growth yesterday?

....

What didn't work yesterday?

....

My goals for today:

☐ .... ☐ ....

☐ .... ☐ ....

"I want to be all that I am capable of becoming."

– Katherine Mansfield

Date: .... | *Today's word:* ....

How am I feeling right now?

....

I'm grateful for…

....

....

....

Why is it worth waking up today?

....

What did I do for my growth yesterday?

....

What didn't work yesterday?

....

My goals for today:

☐ .... ☐ ....

☐ .... ☐ ....

"Whoever is happy
will make others
happy."

— Anne Frank

Date: ....   *Today's word:*........................

How am I feeling right now?

....

I'm grateful for...

....

....

....

Why is it worth waking up today?

....

What did I do for my growth yesterday?

....

What didn't work yesterday?

....

My goals for today:

☐ ....   ☐ ....

☐ ....   ☐ ....

Weekly Check-in

··

How satisfied am I with my previous week?

0   1   2   3   4   5   6   7   8   9   10

What did I learn from this week?

··

··

··

··

What do I want to achieve next week?

··

··

··

··

"Life must be
lived as play."

— Plato

Date: .... Today's word: ....

How am I feeling right now?

....

I'm grateful for…

....

....

....

Why is it worth waking up today?

....

What did I do for my growth yesterday?

....

What didn't work yesterday?

....

My goals for today:

☐ ....   ☐ ....

☐ ....   ☐ ....

"Our life is what our thoughts make it."

– Marcus Aurelius

Date: ....   Today's word:........................

How am I feeling right now?

....

I'm grateful for...

....

....

....

Why is it worth waking up today?

....

What did I do for my growth yesterday?

....

What didn't work yesterday?

....

My goals for today:

☐ ....   ☐ ....

☐ ....   ☐ ....

"What is right to be done cannot be done too soon."

– Jane Austen

Date: .... *Today's word:* ....

How am I feeling right now?

....

I'm grateful for...

....

....

....

Why is it worth waking up today?

....

What did I do for my growth yesterday?

....

What didn't work yesterday?

....

My goals for today:

☐ .... ☐ ....

☐ .... ☐ ....

"Memory is the diary that we all carry about with us."

– Oscar Wilde

Date: ....   *Today's word:*........................

How am I feeling right now?

....

I'm grateful for…

....

....

....

Why is it worth waking up today?

....

What did I do for my growth yesterday?

....

What didn't work yesterday?

....

My goals for today:

☐ ....   ☐ ....

☐ ....   ☐ ....

"A minute's success pays the failure of years."

– Robert Browning

Date: ....   *Today's word:*..........................

How am I feeling right now?

....

I'm grateful for…

....

....

....

Why is it worth waking up today?

....

What did I do for my growth yesterday?

....

What didn't work yesterday?

....

My goals for today:

☐ ....   ☐ ....

☐ ....   ☐ ....

"Beware the
barrenness of
a busy life."

– Socrates

Date: .... | *Today's word:* ....

How am I feeling right now?

....

I'm grateful for…

....

....

....

Why is it worth waking up today?

....

What did I do for my growth yesterday?

....

What didn't work yesterday?

....

My goals for today:

☐ .... ☐ ....

☐ .... ☐ ....

"Start by doing what's necessary; then do what's possible; and suddenly you are doing the impossible."

– Francis of Assisi

Date: .... *Today's word:* ....

How am I feeling right now?

....

I'm grateful for…

....

....

....

Why is it worth waking up today?

....

What did I do for my growth yesterday?

....

What didn't work yesterday?

....

My goals for today:

☐ .... ☐ ....

☐ .... ☐ ....

Weekly Check-in

How satisfied am I with my previous week?

0   1   2   3   4   5   6   7   8   9   10

What did I learn from this week?

....

....

....

....

What do I want to achieve next week?

....

....

....

....

"Find ecstasy in life;
the mere sense of
living is joy enough."

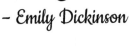
– Emily Dickinson

Date: ....   *Today's word:* ....

How am I feeling right now?

....

I'm grateful for…

....

....

....

Why is it worth waking up today?

....

What did I do for my growth yesterday?

....

What didn't work yesterday?

....

My goals for today:

☐ ....   ☐ ....

☐ ....   ☐ ....

"Time stays long
enough for anyone
who will use it."

– Leonardo da Vinci

Date: .... | *Today's word:* ....

How am I feeling right now?

....

I'm grateful for…

....

....

....

Why is it worth waking up today?

....

What did I do for my growth yesterday?

....

What didn't work yesterday?

....

My goals for today:

☐ .... ☐ ....

☐ .... ☐ ....

"While others prayed for the good time coming, I worked for it."

– Victoria Woodhull

Date: .... | *Today's word:* ....

How am I feeling right now?

....

I'm grateful for...

....

....

....

Why is it worth waking up today?

....

What did I do for my growth yesterday?

....

What didn't work yesterday?

....

My goals for today:

☐ .... ☐ ....

☐ .... ☐ ....

"Be happy for this moment. This moment is your life."

– Omar Khayyam

Date: .... | *Today's word:* ....

How am I feeling right now?

....

I'm grateful for…

....

....

....

Why is it worth waking up today?

....

What did I do for my growth yesterday?

....

What didn't work yesterday?

....

My goals for today:

☐ ....   ☐ ....

☐ ....   ☐ ....

"Adventure is worthwhile in itself."

– Amelia Earhart

Date: ....   *Today's word:* ....

How am I feeling right now?

....

I'm grateful for…

....

....

....

Why is it worth waking up today?

....

What did I do for my growth yesterday?

....

What didn't work yesterday?

....

My goals for today:

☐ ....   ☐ ....

☐ ....   ☐ ....

"To begin, begin."

– William Wordsworth

Date: .... | *Today's word:* ....

How am I feeling right now?

....

I'm grateful for...

....

....

....

Why is it worth waking up today?

....

What did I do for my growth yesterday?

....

What didn't work yesterday?

....

My goals for today:

☐ .... ☐ ....

☐ .... ☐ ....

"Nothing is worth more than this day."

– Johann Wolfgang von Goethe

Date: .... *Today's word:* ....

How am I feeling right now?

....

I'm grateful for...

....

....

....

Why is it worth waking up today?

....

What did I do for my growth yesterday?

....

What didn't work yesterday?

....

My goals for today:

☐ .... ☐ ....

☐ .... ☐ ....

Weekly Check-in

How satisfied am I with my previous week?

0   1   2   3   4   5   6   7   8   9   10

What did I learn from this week?

....

....

....

....

What do I want to achieve next week?

....

....

....

....

"My best friend is the one who brings out the best in me."

– Henry Ford

Date: ....   *Today's word:* ....

How am I feeling right now?

....

I'm grateful for…

....

....

....

Why is it worth waking up today?

....

What did I do for my growth yesterday?

....

What didn't work yesterday?

....

My goals for today:

☐ ....   ☐ ....

☐ ....   ☐ ....

"No."

— Rosa Parks

Date: .... | *Today's word:* ....

How am I feeling right now?

....

I'm grateful for...

....

....

....

Why is it worth waking up today?

....

What did I do for my growth yesterday?

....

What didn't work yesterday?

....

My goals for today:

☐ .... ☐ ....

☐ .... ☐ ....

"The beginning is always today."

– Mary Wollstonecraft

Date: .... *Today's word:*........................

How am I feeling right now?

....

I'm grateful for...

....

....

....

Why is it worth waking up today?

....

What did I do for my growth yesterday?

....

What didn't work yesterday?

....

My goals for today:

☐ .... ☐ ....

☐ .... ☐ ....

"The energy of the
mind is the essence
of life."

– Aristotle

Date: .... | *Today's word:* ....

How am I feeling right now?

....

I'm grateful for…

....

....

....

Why is it worth waking up today?

....

What did I do for my growth yesterday?

....

What didn't work yesterday?

....

My goals for today:

☐ .... ☐ ....

☐ .... ☐ ....

"A friend is a gift you give yourself."

– Robert Louis Stevenson

Date: .... | *Today's word:* ....

How am I feeling right now?

....

I'm grateful for…

....

....

....

Why is it worth waking up today?

....

What did I do for my growth yesterday?

....

What didn't work yesterday?

....

My goals for today:

☐ .... ☐ ....

☐ .... ☐ ....

"I will prepare and someday my chance will come."

– Abraham Lincoln

Date: .... | *Today's word:* ....

How am I feeling right now?

....

I'm grateful for…

....

....

....

Why is it worth waking up today?

....

What did I do for my growth yesterday?

....

What didn't work yesterday?

....

My goals for today:

☐ .... ☐ ....

☐ .... ☐ ....

"Let the beauty of what you love be what you do."

– Rumi

Date: .... | *Today's word:*.....................

How am I feeling right now?

....

I'm grateful for...

....

....

....

Why is it worth waking up today?

....

What did I do for my growth yesterday?

....

What didn't work yesterday?

....

My goals for today:

☐ .... ☐ ....

☐ .... ☐ ....

Weekly Check-in

· ·

How satisfied am I with my previous week?

0   1   2   3   4   5   6   7   8   9   10

What did I learn from this week?

....

....

....

....

What do I want to achieve next week?

....

....

....

....

"*Life is largely a matter of expectation.*"

— Horace

Date: .... *Today's word:*......................

How am I feeling right now?

....

I'm grateful for…

....

....

....

Why is it worth waking up today?

....

What did I do for my growth yesterday?

....

What didn't work yesterday?

....

My goals for today:

☐ .... ☐ ....

☐ .... ☐ ....

"Friendships are discovered rather than made."

– Harriet Beecher Stowe

Date: .... | *Today's word:* ....

How am I feeling right now?

....

I'm grateful for…

....

....

....

Why is it worth waking up today?

....

What did I do for my growth yesterday?

....

What didn't work yesterday?

....

My goals for today:

☐ .... ☐ ....

☐ .... ☐ ....

"Certain things catch
your eye, but pursue
only those that capture
the heart."

– Ancient Indian Proverb

Date: .... *Today's word:*......................

How am I feeling right now?

....

I'm grateful for...

....

....

....

Why is it worth waking up today?

....

What did I do for my growth yesterday?

....

What didn't work yesterday?

....

My goals for today:

☐ .... ☐ ....

☐ .... ☐ ....

"The only person you are destined to become is the person you decide to be."

– Ralph Waldo Emerson

Date: ....   *Today's word:* ....

How am I feeling right now?

....

I'm grateful for…

....

....

....

Why is it worth waking up today?

....

What did I do for my growth yesterday?

....

What didn't work yesterday?

....

My goals for today:

☐ ....   ☐ ....

☐ ....   ☐ ....

"We can easily forgive a child who is afraid of the dark; the real tragedy of life is when men are afraid of the light."

– Plato

Date: .... *Today's word:* ....

How am I feeling right now?

....

I'm grateful for…

....

....

....

Why is it worth waking up today?

....

What did I do for my growth yesterday?

....

What didn't work yesterday?

....

My goals for today:

☐ .... ☐ ....

☐ .... ☐ ....

"How wonderful it is that nobody need wait a single moment before starting to improve the world."

– Anne Frank

Date: .... *Today's word:* ....

How am I feeling right now?

....

I'm grateful for...

....

....

....

Why is it worth waking up today?

....

What did I do for my growth yesterday?

....

What didn't work yesterday?

....

My goals for today:

☐ ....   ☐ ....

☐ ....   ☐ ....

"Everything you've
ever wanted is on the
other side of fear."

– George Adair

Date: .... | *Today's word:* ....

How am I feeling right now?

....

I'm grateful for...

....

....

....

Why is it worth waking up today?

....

What did I do for my growth yesterday?

....

What didn't work yesterday?

....

My goals for today:

☐ .... ☐ ....

☐ .... ☐ ....

Weekly Check-in

How satisfied am I with my previous week?

0   1   2   3   4   5   6   7   8   9   10

What did I learn from this week?

....

....

....

....

What do I want to achieve next week?

....

....

....

....

Running Out Of Pages?

We hope you love Morning Mindset as much as we do and it's been helping you feeling happier and calmer every day.

Order the next journal now from
GritJournals.com

"A disciplined mind
brings happiness."

– The Buddha

Date:........................ *Today's word:*........................

How am I feeling right now?

....

I'm grateful for...

....

....

....

Why is it worth waking up today?

....

What did I do for my growth yesterday?

....

What didn't work yesterday?

....

My goals for today:

☐ .... ☐ ....

☐ .... ☐ ....

"What we achieve inwardly will change outer reality."

– Plutarch

Date: .... | *Today's word:* ....

How am I feeling right now?

....

I'm grateful for…

....

....

....

Why is it worth waking up today?

....

What did I do for my growth yesterday?

....

What didn't work yesterday?

....

My goals for today:

☐ .... ☐ ....

☐ .... ☐ ....

"When everything seems to be going against you, remember that the airplane takes off against the wind, not with it."

– Henry Ford

Date: .... | *Today's word:* ....

How am I feeling right now?

....

I'm grateful for…

....

....

....

Why is it worth waking up today?

....

What did I do for my growth yesterday?

....

What didn't work yesterday?

....

My goals for today:

☐ .... ☐ ....

☐ .... ☐ ....

"The most difficult thing is the decision to act, the rest is merely tenacity."

– Amelia Earhart

Date: .... *Today's word:* ....

How am I feeling right now?

....

I'm grateful for...

....

....

....

Why is it worth waking up today?

....

What did I do for my growth yesterday?

....

What didn't work yesterday?

....

My goals for today:

☐ .... ☐ ....

☐ .... ☐ ....

"Simplicity is the ultimate sophistication."

– Leonardo da Vinci

Date: .... | *Today's word:* ....

How am I feeling right now?

....

I'm grateful for…

....

....

....

Why is it worth waking up today?

....

What did I do for my growth yesterday?

....

What didn't work yesterday?

....

My goals for today:

☐ .... ☐ ....

☐ .... ☐ ....

"Know yourself to improve yourself."

– Auguste Comte

Date: .... | *Today's word:* ....

How am I feeling right now?

....

I'm grateful for…

....

....

....

Why is it worth waking up today?

....

What did I do for my growth yesterday?

....

What didn't work yesterday?

....

My goals for today:

☐ .... ☐ ....

☐ .... ☐ ....

"Radiate boundless love towards the entire world."

– The Buddha

Date: .... *Today's word:* ....

How am I feeling right now?

....

I'm grateful for…

....

....

....

Why is it worth waking up today?

....

What did I do for my growth yesterday?

....

What didn't work yesterday?

....

My goals for today:

☐ .... ☐ ....

☐ .... ☐ ....

Weekly Check-in

How satisfied am I with my previous week?

0   1   2   3   4   5   6   7   8   9   10

What did I learn from this week?

....

....

....

....

What do I want to achieve next week?

....

....

....

....

ABOUT GRIT JOURNALS

We believe that you can achieve anything in your life with grit: daily practice, determination, resilience, consistency and passion.

The purpose of our journals is to help you get in the grit mindset every single day to become the best version of yourself and create the life you want.

Find out more at **gritjournals.com**

Made in the USA
Las Vegas, NV
27 October 2020